DEMETER & PERSEPHONE

SPRING HELD HOSTAGE

A GREEK MYTH

OSIDG

STORY BY
JUSTINE & RON FONTES

PENCILS BY
STEVE KURTH

INKS BY
BARBARA SCHULZ

EUROPE

MEDITERRANEAN SEA

NORTH AFRICA

DEMETER & PERSEPHONE

SPRING HELD HOSTAGE

A GREEK MYTH

GREECE

MOUNT OLYMPUS ▲

IONIAN SEA

AEGEAN SEA

ELEUSIS

ATHENS

GRAPHIC UNIVERSE™

Demeter is one of the most important figures in Greek mythology. She is the goddess of farming (especially corn and grains) and of the harvest. For the ancient Greeks, the story of Demeter's search for her kidnapped daughter Persephone explains the cycle of seasons. Persephone's reunion with her mother represents the beginning of springtime — the return of warm weather and budding crops. For more than two thousand years, followers of Demeter celebrated the harvest of those crops in secret rituals at the goddess's temple in Eleusis, Greece.

In retelling Demeter's story, Justine and Ron Fontes used classical and modern sources such as Ovid's *Metamorphoses* and Edith Hamilton's *Mythology*. Artist Steve Kurth used classical Greek art and anthropological sources to create the visual details. And David Mulroy of the University of Wisconsin-Milwaukee ensured historical and visual accuracy.

STORY BY JUSTINE AND RON FONTES

PENCILS BY STEVE KURTH

INKS BY BARBARA SCHULZ

COLOURING AND LETTERING BY RAY DILLON OF GOLDEN GOAT STUDIOS

CONSULTANT: DAVID MULROY,
UNIVERSITY OF WISCONSIN-MILWAUKEE

Copyright © 2007 by Lerner Publishing Group, Inc.

Graphic Universe™ is a trademark of Lerner Publishing Group, Inc.

This book was first published in the USA in 2007. First published in the UK in 2008 by Lerner Books, Dalton House, 60 Windsor Avenue, London SW19 2RR

Website address: www.lernerbooks.co.uk

This edition was updated and edited for UK publication by Discovery Books Ltd., Unit 3, 37 Watling Street, Leintwardine, Shropshire SY7 0LW

British Library Cataloguing in Publication Data

Fontes, Justine
   Demeter and Persephone : spring held hostage. - (Graphic myths and legends series)
      1. Demeter (Greek deity) - Comic books, strips, etc. - Juvenile fiction 2. Persephone (Greek deity) - Comic books, strips, etc. - Juvenile fiction 3. Children's stories -Comic books, strips, etc.
      I. Title II. Fontes, Ron III. Kurth, Steve IV. Schultz, Barbara, 1948-
      741.5

   ISBN-13: 978 1 58013 318 0

Printed in China

TABLE OF CONTENTS

A WINTERLESS WORLD

ACCORDING TO THE ANCIENT GREEKS, THERE WAS A TIME WHEN WINTER DIDN'T EXIST. LEAVES STAYED ON THE TREES ALL YEAR. FLOWERS WERE ALWAYS IN BLOOM. THE FIELDS WERE ALWAYS FERTILE.

FOR THIS, THE GREEKS THANKED THE GODDESS DEMETER AND HER ONLY CHILD, THE BEAUTIFUL PERSEPHONE.

WE SHARE THE FIRST LOAF BAKED FROM THE NEW GRAIN IN GRATITUDE TO DEMETER!

WE THANK YOU, DEMETER, FOR OUR FERTILE FIELDS!

WE THANK YOU, DEMETER, AS WE DO EVERY DAY WITH EVERY TASK!

WE THANK YOU, DEMETER AND PERSEPHONE, FOR THIS BOUNTY!

HADES SOMETIMES VISITED EARTH OR MOUNT OLYMPUS WITHOUT ANYONE KNOWING. HE OWNED A MAGIC HELMET THAT MADE HIM INVISIBLE.

A HANDY HAT INDEED!

NOW I CAN WATCH MY FAVOURITE MAIDEN AT PLAY. AH, *PERSEPHONE*! SHE IS MORE BEAUTIFUL THAN EVERY FLOWER IN THIS SUNNY MEADOW.

ONE DAY, ZEUS VISITED HADES IN HIS UNDERGROUND PALACE.

SO, BROTHER, HOW ARE THINGS ON MOUNT OLYMPUS?

GOOD, EXCEPT THAT EVERYONE MISSES YOU.

MY MANY DUTIES KEEP ME BUSY. BUT I HAVE ALSO GROWN ACCUSTOMED TO THE UNDERWORLD.

THEN YOU ARE HAPPY?

I WOULD BE, IF ONLY I HAD A *QUEEN* TO SHARE MY DOMAIN.

TO MY EYES, ONE MAID STANDS ABOVE ALL OTHERS— PERSEPHONE.

THEN WHAT ARE YOU WAITING FOR? YOU SHALL HAVE HER!

HMM, MAYBE I SHOULD HAVE ASKED DEMETER AND PERSEPHONE FIRST.

THANKS, ZEUS! YOU'RE THE GREATEST.

YES, WELL, GOOD LUCK WITH THAT.

IF I TELL DEMETER NOW, THERE'LL BE ALL KINDS OF *TROUBLE*. IF I JUST LET THINGS RUN THEIR COURSE ...

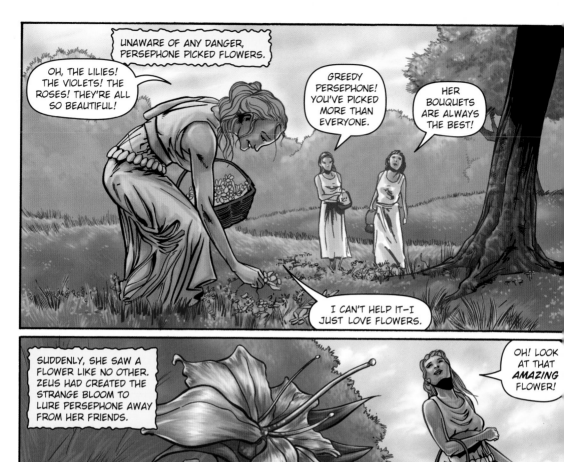

UNAWARE OF ANY DANGER, PERSEPHONE PICKED FLOWERS.

OH, THE LILIES! THE VIOLETS! THE ROSES! THEY'RE ALL SO BEAUTIFUL!

GREEDY PERSEPHONE! YOU'VE PICKED MORE THAN EVERYONE.

HER BOUQUETS ARE ALWAYS THE BEST!

I CAN'T HELP IT—I JUST LOVE FLOWERS.

SUDDENLY, SHE SAW A FLOWER LIKE NO OTHER. ZEUS HAD CREATED THE STRANGE BLOOM TO LURE PERSEPHONE AWAY FROM HER FRIENDS.

OH! LOOK AT THAT *AMAZING* FLOWER!

I KNOW I SHOULDN'T WANDER OFF ALONE. BUT I MUST HAVE IT FOR THE CENTRE OF MY BOUQUET!

PERSEPHONE, WHERE ARE YOU GOING?

STAY WITH US!

11

JUST AS PERSEPHONE REACHED FOR THE FLOWER, THE EARTH OPENED!

WHAT'S HAPPENING?

UNDERGROUND HORSES?!

HYA! HYA! FASTER!

HADES! I THOUGHT HE NEVER LEFT THE UNDERWORLD.

NO!!!

YOU CANNOT ESCAPE ME, MY FAIR QUEEN!

IGNORING PERSEPHONE'S PLEAS, HADES DROVE ON TOWARDS A BEAUTIFUL POOL.

THE DARK DOMAIN

HADES DROVE HIS CHARIOT DOWN THROUGH THE POOL ...

HYA! HYA!

HELP!!!

... INTO HIS KINGDOM BELOW.

MY BELT! LOST—AS AM I. CAN HADES REALLY MEAN TO KEEP ME HERE?

WELCOME TO MY KINGDOM.

YOU MUST LET ME GO! PLEASE, BY THE GODS, I *BEG* YOU! I CANNOT LIVE AMONG THE *DEAD*!

WHAT UGLY PLANTS: WEEPING WILLOWS AND ASPHODEL, THE WEED THAT GROWS ON GRAVES. EVEN THE POPLARS LOOK BLACK AND SICKLY.

IS THAT A THREE-HEADED DOG OR SOME KIND OF DRAGON?

WOOF WOOF!

ARF ARF!

BOW WOW!

THERE'S MY GOOD BOY! WHO'S THE BEST DOG IN THE UNDERWORLD? THAT'S CERBERUS!

PLEASE DON'T WORRY. CERBERUS WON'T HURT ANYONE—UNLESS THEY TRY TO LEAVE.

SEE, HE LIKES YOU.

THIS HIDEOUS MONSTER IS HIS *PET*?

ALMOST AS MUCH AS I DO.

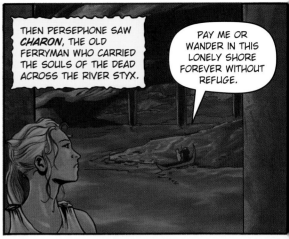

THEN PERSEPHONE SAW *CHARON*, THE OLD FERRYMAN WHO CARRIED THE SOULS OF THE DEAD ACROSS THE RIVER STYX.

PAY ME OR WANDER IN THIS LONELY SHORE FOREVER WITHOUT REFUGE.

THAT'S MORE LIKE IT.

PLEASE FORGIVE CHARON. HE MUST BE PAID FOR HIS DREARY WORK, OR HE WILL NOT DO IT.

THAT'S UNDERSTANDABLE. EVEN ABOVE, NO FERRYMAN LIKES TO WORK FOR NOTHING.

YOU ARE MOST KIND. I HOPE YOU COME TO UNDERSTAND ALL THOSE YOU MEET HERE. SO FEW PEOPLE APPRECIATE THE DARKER SIDE OF LIFE.

THOSE ARE HARDLY THE WORDS OF A BRUTE, BUT ...

CHARON WILL BE BACK SOON TO TAKE US ACROSS.

BUT SHE'S *ALIVE*!

YES, MY LORD HADES.

AND SHE IS MY GUEST. OBEY OR EXPERIENCE THINGS *WORSE THAN DEATH*.

15

HOW STRANGE TO SEE THIS GLOOMY RIVER WITH MY OWN EYES. UP TIL NOW, I'VE ONLY HEARD THE GODS SWEAR 'BY THE STYX'.

MY KINGDOM HAS MANY RIVERS. BUT THE STYX IS THE LONGEST. IT SURROUNDS THE UNDERWORLD WITH NINE LOOPS.

DID HE KIDNAP ME TO GIVE ME A TOUR?

SHADES MUST CROSS THE STYX TO ENTER MY KINGDOM.

PERHAPS YOU ARE HUNGRY OR THIRSTY. MY PALACE IS NOT FAR.

OH NO! HE CAN'T TRICK ME. IF I EAT OR DRINK ANYTHING DOWN HERE, I'LL HAVE TO STAY FOREVER.

NO, THANK YOU.

SHE'LL GET HUNGRY EVENTUALLY.

I CAN BE PATIENT.

HERE ARE THE KINGS WHO HELP ME DECIDE WHETHER A SHADE GOES TO TARTARUS OR THE ELYSIAN FIELDS OR REMAINS HERE IN ACHERON.

I HAVE HEARD OF AEACUS, MINOS, AND RHADAMANTHYS. WE ARE ALL CHILDREN OF ZEUS. BUT I HAVE NEVER MET THEM BEFORE.

THEN PERHAPS YOU WOULD LIKE TO MEET THE SHADES OF SOME OF THE GREATEST MEN WHO EVER LIVED.

GENTLEMEN, I WOULD LIKE TO INTRODUCE MY MOST HONOURED GUEST, PERSEPHONE, THE DAUGHTER OF ZEUS AND DEMETER.

HE DRAGS ME HERE LIKE A SACK OF OLIVES, THEN CALLS ME AN *HONOURED* GUEST?!

DELIGHTED TO MEET YOU.

AN HONOUR TO MEET THE DAUGHTER OF SUCH A GREAT GODDESS.

YOU WARM THIS DULL REGION LIKE A RAY OF SUNSHINE.

FEW LIVING BEINGS HAD EVER BEEN WHERE PERSEPHONE STOOD.

I SUPPOSE IT COULDN'T HURT TO BE POLITE.

PLEASE TELL ME ABOUT YOUR WORK.

WE READ EACH SHADE'S SCROLL.

WE WEIGH THE DEEDS OF HIS LIFETIME.

AND WITH HADES' HELP, WE DECIDE THE SHADE'S FATE FOR *ETERNITY*.

DO MORE SHADES GO TO TARTARUS OR THE ELYSIAN FIELDS?

MOST SOULS ARE NEITHER BAD ENOUGH TO DESERVE TARTARUS NOR GOOD ENOUGH FOR THE ELYSIAN FIELDS. MOST SIMPLY WANDER ACHERON AS SHADOWS OF THEIR FORMER SELVES. THEY CANNOT THINK OR SPEAK BUT MINDLESSLY PERFORM THE TASKS THEY LOVED IN LIFE.

17

ARE THOSE THE **FURIES?**

YES, BUT YOU HAVE NOTHING TO FEAR FROM THE KINDLY ONES. THEY ONLY PUNISH THE GUILTY.

IN THE WORLD ABOVE, THERE IS OFTEN GREAT INJUSTICE. CRIMES GO UNPUNISHED AND GOODNESS UNREWARDED. BUT HERE THE WRONGS ARE RIGHTED.

19

ONLY THE WORST CRIMINALS WIND UP IN TARTARUS. FEW CRIMES MERIT ETERNAL TORTURE.

THIS MAN'S NAME HAS COME TO DESCRIBE HIS TORTURE— TO BE *TEASED* BY *DESIRE*.

TANTALUS!

CORRECT, MY BRILLIANT ND BEAUTIFUL QUEEN!

IN LIFE, TANTALUS WAS A KING WHO RECEIVED GREAT FAVOURS FROM THE GODS. BUT THE UNGRATEFUL WRETCH COMMITTED MANY CRIMES, INCLUDING *KILLING* HIS OWN SON!

HERE HIS THIRST FOR POWER AND HUNGER FOR WEALTH ARE CONSTANTLY PUNISHED.

THE WATER RECEDES FROM HIS LIPS! FRUIT FLEES HIS GRASP!

HE CAN NEVER DRINK, NEVER EAT. TANTALUS WILL ALWAYS WANT AND NEVER HAVE.

SISYPHUS WAS ALSO A KING. YET DESPITE ALL HIS RICHES, HE CHEATED FOR MORE.

SO MANY MORTALS FALL FOR GREED!

HERE HE ENDLESSLY PUSHES THAT HUGE BLOCK UP THAT STEEP HILL. WHEN THE ROCK REACHES THE TOP, IT SLIDES BACK DOWN AND SISYPHUS MUST START ALL OVER AGAIN.

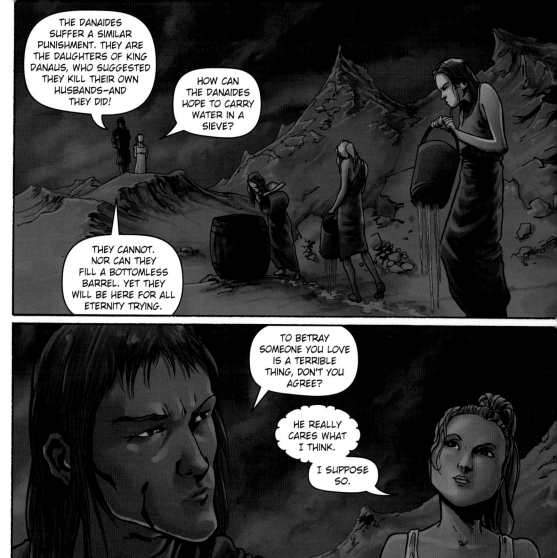

THE DANAIDES SUFFER A SIMILAR PUNISHMENT. THEY ARE THE DAUGHTERS OF KING DANAUS, WHO SUGGESTED THEY KILL THEIR OWN HUSBANDS—AND THEY DID!

HOW CAN THE DANAIDES HOPE TO CARRY WATER IN A SIEVE?

THEY CANNOT. NOR CAN THEY FILL A BOTTOMLESS BARREL. YET THEY WILL BE HERE FOR ALL ETERNITY TRYING.

TO BETRAY SOMEONE YOU LOVE IS A TERRIBLE THING, DON'T YOU AGREE?

HE REALLY CARES WHAT I THINK.

I SUPPOSE SO.

BUT YOU HAVE SEEN ENOUGH OF THE CRUEL SIDE OF MY KINGDOM. MAY I SHOW YOU WHERE THE SHADES OF THE VERY BEST PEOPLE GO?

I SHOULD BE FURIOUS WITH HADES. BUT HIS TOUCH IS GENTLE, AND I DO NOT SEE EVIL IN HIS EYES, ONLY SADNESS.

EVERY PLEASURE OF THE WORLD ABOVE IS ENJOYED HERE FOR ETERNITY BY THOSE WHO LED GOOD LIVES.

I HOPED YOU WOULD THINK SO.

IF ONLY SHE COULD *WANT* TO BE MY QUEEN! WITH PERSEPHONE AT MY SIDE, THIS REALM WOULD BE A PARADISE.

THE FLOWERS! OH, AND THE STRANGE PURPLE GLOW. IT'S ALMOST MORE BEAUTIFUL THAN SUNLIGHT!

AT FIRST, ONLY CHILDREN OF THE GODS COULD ENTER THE ELYSIAN FIELDS. BUT NOW WE HOST GREAT HEROES, POETS AND OTHER MORTALS WHOSE EXCELLENT DEEDS ATTRACT THE FAVOUR OF THE GODS.

I SING OF THE BRAVEST MAN TO EVER LIFT A SWORD ...

THIS CERTAINLY BEATS BEING IN BATTLE!

NO RAIN OR STORMS EVER DISTURB THIS BLISS.

I HOPE SHE CAN BE HAPPY HERE. I COULDN'T BEAR TO SEE PERSEPHONE SAD.

HE HAS ALL OF ZEUS'S POWER BUT WITH A GENTLE SADNESS. PERHAPS THAT COMES FROM THE CONSTANT REMINDER THAT LIFE IS FLEETING.

WE COULD SPEND MANY A PLEASANT HOUR HERE. BUT THERE IS MORE FOR YOU TO SEE.

MANY PEOPLE THINK THAT I AM DEATH. BUT THAT IS NOT TRUE. THIS HANDSOME YOUNG SPIRIT HAS THAT DUBIOUS HONOUR.

THANATOS, THIS IS PERSEPHONE.

AT YOUR SERVICE.

NO WONDER THE KING LOVES HER!

THANATOS LIVES WITH HIS BROTHER, HYPNOS.

MY JOB IS TO MAKE MORTALS SLEEP.

LOOK HOW HADES SMILES AT HER. THE LORD OF THE DEAD IS IN LOVE!

THIS IS MY SON, MORPHEUS, THE GOD OF DREAMS.

PLEASED TO MEET YOU.

WOULD YOU LIKE TO SEE THE GATES THROUGH WHICH DREAMS ENTER THE WORLD?

YES, THANK YOU.

THIS HAS TO BE THE STRANGEST DAY I'VE EVER SPENT! BUT WITH ANY LUCK, MOTHER WILL FIND ME BEFORE THIS TOUR ENDS.

I SEND IDLE OR DECEPTIVE DREAMS THROUGH THE IVORY GATE.

DREAMS THAT TELL THE TRUTH OR POINT TO THE FUTURE GO THROUGH THE GATE MADE OF HORN.

WHAT IF ALL THIS IS A DREAM AND I'LL WAKE UP IN THE SUNNY MEADOW?

I SUDDENLY FEEL TIRED AND HUNGRY. I WANT TO GO *HOME!*

A WORRIED MOTHER

WHILE PERSEPHONE TOURED THE UNDERWORLD, DEMETER FRANTICALLY SEARCHED THE MEADOW. SHE HAD HEARD HER DAUGHTER SCREAM.

PERSEPHONE'S IN *TROUBLE!*

DEMETER THREW ON A VEIL THAT MADE HER FLY LIKE A BIRD.

I MUST FIND HER!

FOR NINE DAYS, DEMETER FLEW THE WORLD, SEARCHING FOR HER DAUGHTER.

PERSEPHONE AND HER FRIENDS WERE PICKING FLOWERS HERE.

WHAT COULD HAVE MADE PERSEPHONE SCREAM?

I WILL NOT REST UNTIL I SEE HER AGAIN!

WHERE CAN PERSEPHONE BE?!

25

ON THE TENTH DAY, DEMETER MET HECATE, THE GODDESS OF WITCHCRAFT.

YOU ARE LOOKING FOR PERSEPHONE?

YES! HAVE YOU SEEN HER?

SOMEONE TOOK HER. BUT I DON'T KNOW WHO. TRY ASKING HELIOS. HE SEES ALL.

OF COURSE! I SHOULD HAVE ASKED HIM SOONER! THANK YOU, HECATE.

SO DEMETER FLEW UP TO THE SKY, WHERE SHE FOUND THE SUN DRIVING HIS GOLDEN CHARIOT.

HAIL, HELIOS! HAVE YOU SEEN PERSEPHONE?

HADES TOOK HER TO THE UNDERWORLD.

HADES! NO WONDER I HAVEN'T SEEN HER ANYWHERE ON EARTH.

I BET ZEUS IS BEHIND ALL THIS. HE MAKES ME SO FURIOUS!

DID YOU SEE WHERE THEY WENT?

BUT THE IMPORTANT THING NOW IS TO RESCUE PERSEPHONE!

TRY THE NYMPH CYANE'S POOL.

THANK YOU, HELIOS.

SOON DEMETER REACHED THE POOL.

CYANE! CYANE!

THE NYMPH IS GONE! BUT WHAT'S THAT FLOATING ON THE WATER?

PERSEPHONE'S BELT!

THEN IT'S ALL TRUE! HADES *KIDNAPPED* MY DAUGHTER!

BY THE STYX, I SWEAR I WILL BRING HER BACK!

DEMETER WENT STRAIGHT TO ZEUS.

YOU MUST MAKE HADES *RETURN* PERSEPHONE! HOW COULD YOU GIVE AWAY MY ONLY CHILD?

I WAS JUST TRYING TO MAKE MY BROTHER HAPPY.

THERE'S NOTHING I CAN DO. YOU MUST UNDERSTAND.

ARE YOU SAYING THE KING OF THE GODS IS *HELPLESS*?

THIS IS WHAT MY HUSBAND'S UNFAITHFULNESS BRINGS— MOTHERS AND CHILDREN ALWAYS TURNING UP FOR FAVOURS.

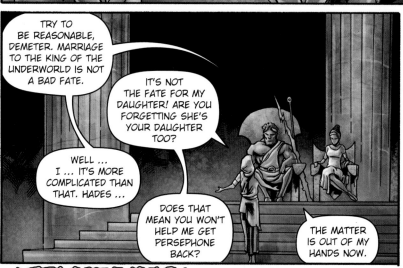

TRY TO BE REASONABLE, DEMETER. MARRIAGE TO THE KING OF THE UNDERWORLD IS NOT A BAD FATE.

IT'S NOT THE FATE FOR MY DAUGHTER! ARE YOU FORGETTING SHE'S YOUR DAUGHTER TOO?

WELL ... I ... IT'S MORE COMPLICATED THAN THAT. HADES ...

DOES THAT MEAN YOU WON'T HELP ME GET PERSEPHONE BACK?

THE MATTER IS OUT OF MY HANDS NOW.

I WON'T STAY ON MOUNT OLYMPUS ANOTHER *MINUTE* I WOULD RATHER BE AMONG THE FOOLISH MORTALS THAN THE PITILESS GODS.

SOMETIMES THE GODS DISGUISED THEMSELVES AS MORTALS.

THE MORTALS MAY SOMEHOW HELP ME RESCUE PERSEPHONE— OR AT LEAST DISTRACT ME FROM MY GRIEF UNTIL I CAN FORM A PLAN.

GODS AND GODDESSES DRANK NECTAR AND LIVED ON A FOOD CALLED AMBROSIA.

THIS HEAT AND DUST! I FEEL LIKE I'M WILTING. SMALL WONDER, I HAVEN'T TASTED AMBROSIA OR NECTAR SINCE PERSEPHONE DISAPPEARED.

WELCOME... STRANGER!

DIVINE RADIANCE IN MY DOORWAY!

WELCOME TO OUR HOME.

WE MUST BE VERY CAREFUL. CONTACT WITH THE GODS CAN BRING LUCK—OR DISASTER!

WE TOLD HER THERE MIGHT BE WORK IN OUR HOUSE.

OR AT LEAST A HOT MEAL.

OF COURSE! I'M SURE WE COULD USE ... A NANNY.

YES, YOUNG DEMOPHOON NEEDS A NURSE.

OUR BABY SON IN THE HANDS OF A GODDESS!

DEMETER DECIDED TO RAISE DEMOPHOON LIKE A GOD. INSTEAD OF FEEDING HIM, SHE BREATHED ON THE BABY!

SHE ANOINTED HIM WITH AMBROSIA, THE FOOD OF THE GODS.

AND EACH NIGHT, DEMETER PUT DEMOPHOON IN THE FIRE TO BURN OFF THE MORTAL PARTS OF HIM.

THERE YOU GO, LITTLE ONE.

COO! GURGLE! COO!

AIYEEEEE! MY BABY!

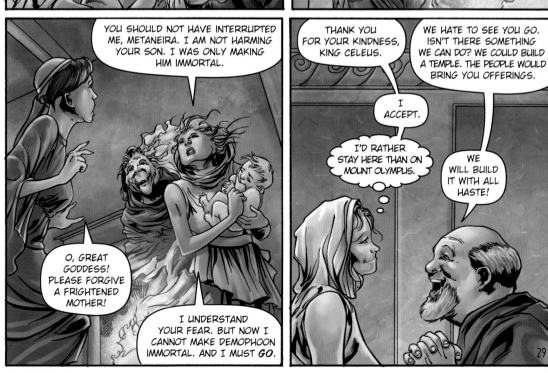

YOU SHOULD NOT HAVE INTERRUPTED ME, METANEIRA. I AM NOT HARMING YOUR SON. I WAS ONLY MAKING HIM IMMORTAL.

O, GREAT GODDESS! PLEASE FORGIVE A FRIGHTENED MOTHER!

I UNDERSTAND YOUR FEAR. BUT NOW I CANNOT MAKE DEMOPHOON IMMORTAL. AND I MUST GO.

THANK YOU FOR YOUR KINDNESS, KING CELEUS.

WE HATE TO SEE YOU GO. ISN'T THERE SOMETHING WE CAN DO? WE COULD BUILD A TEMPLE. THE PEOPLE WOULD BRING YOU OFFERINGS.

I ACCEPT.

I'D RATHER STAY HERE THAN ON MOUNT OLYMPUS.

WE WILL BUILD IT WITH ALL HASTE!

29

ZEUS AND THE OTHER GODS ON MOUNT OLYMPUS HEARD THE PEOPLE'S PRAYERS.

SOMEONE MUST CONVINCE DEMETER TO FIX THE FIELDS! OR WE'LL **ALL** BE RULING THE DEAD LIKE MY BROTHER!

YOU! ALL OF YOU! ONE BY ONE, DO YOUR BEST UNTIL DEMETER ENDS THIS FOOLISH STRIKE!

BY SOMEONE, JUST WHOM DID YOU HAVE IN MIND?

JUST LIKE ZEUS TO SEND US TO DO HIS DIRTY WORK.

I'LL GO! SOMEONE NEEDS TO TALK SOME SENSE INTO HER!

MY TEMPLES ARE EMPTY! NO ONE THINKS OF **LOVE** ANY MORE. ALL THEY WANT IS FOOD.

PERHAPS PERSEPHONE CAN LEARN TO LOVE HADES. I CAN HELP! BUT PLEASE, DEMETER, YOU MUST LET THE MORTALS HAVE FOOD.

NOT UNTIL I HAVE MY DAUGHTER, APHRODITE!

WHAT ELSE CAN I SAY? SHE'S AS STUBBORN AS HERA.

THE **SOLDIERS** ARE ALL TOO HUNGRY AND WEAK TO FIGHT. WITHOUT GRAIN TO FEED THE BULLS, WHAT WILL PEOPLE SACRIFICE TO ME?

I'LL BRING YOU **ANYTHING** YOU WANT: SPOILS OF WAR, GOLD, JEWELS ...

I WANT MY DAUGHTER, ARES! WILL YOU BRING ME PERSEPHONE?

IF YOU DON'T IMPROVE THE FIELDS SOON, THE PEOPLE WILL EAT EVERY LAST FISH IN MY SEAS!

THEN, POSEIDON, YOU WILL BE AS **LONELY** AS I AM WITHOUT PERSEPHONE.

ISN'T THERE ANYTHING I CAN GIVE YOU? PEARLS? MERMAIDS? SUNKEN TREASURES?

GIVE ME BACK MY **DAUGHTER!**

DEMETER, PLEASE HAVE MERCY! **ATHENS IS STARVING!** SURELY YOU CANNOT THINK IT IS WISE TO MAKE THE ENTIRE HUMAN RACE DIE BECAUSE ONE GODDESS WAS TAKEN AGAINST HER WILL.

IF THE GODDESS WERE YOU OR YOUR DAUGHTER, YOU MIGHT FEEL DIFFERENTLY, ATHENA.

THE PEOPLE OF ATHENS COULD BUILD YOU A GREAT TEMPLE.

I DON'T **WANT** ANOTHER TEMPLE. I WANT MY **DAUGHTER!**

IF YOU DON'T MAKE THE CROPS GROW AGAIN SOON, ALL THE ANIMALS WILL BE KILLED FOR FOOD. TO BE HUNTED IS ONE THING, TO BE STARVED AND EATEN INTO EXTINCTION....

ARTEMIS, IF YOU CAN FEEL FOR THE BEASTS OF THE HUNT, WHY CAN'T YOU FEEL FOR MY *DAUGHTER*?

WITHOUT GRAPES, THERE CAN BE *NO WINE*. WOULD YOU DEPRIVE THE WORLD OF SUCH JOY?

AS LONG AS I AM DEPRIVED OF MINE, BACCHUS.

DEMETER, HAVE *MERCY!* THINK OF THE POOR MORTALS WITHOUT WINE TO DRINK!

I CAN ONLY THINK OF MY *DAUGHTER*.

THERE MUST BE SOME WAY TO SHINE THE LIGHT OF *REASON* ON YOUR TROUBLED MIND.

I DON'T NEED MY GIFT OF PROPHECY TO SEE THAT DEMETER HAS MADE UP HER MIND!

IT'S SIMPLE, APOLLO. GET ZEUS TO MAKE HADES RETURN PERSEPHONE.

SURELY, AS A *MOTHER*, YOU MUST FEEL FOR THE MORTALS WHOSE BABES STARVE BECAUSE OF YOUR STUBBORNNESS?

YOUR HUSBAND IS MORE AT FAULT THAN I AM, HERA—AND YOU KNOW IT!

YOU'RE RIGHT. ZEUS SHOULD NEVER HAVE GIVEN AWAY PERSEPHONE WITHOUT FIRST ASKING BOTH OF YOU. BUT WHAT CAN WE DO *NOW*?

FINALLY, ZEUS CALLED HERMES, THE MESSENGER OF THE GODS.

EVERYONE HAS TRIED TO CHANGE DEMETER'S MIND. BUT IT'S CLEAR SHE'LL LET THE WORLD STARVE IF WE DON'T GET PERSEPHONE BACK.

THAT'S WHY I WANT YOU TO GO DOWN TO THE UNDERWORLD AND *BRING BACK THE GIRL*.

A GODDESS CAN BE EVEN MORE STUBBORN THAN A MORTAL MOTHER.

HADES WON'T LIKE THIS, BUT HE'LL HAVE TO UNDERSTAND.

THE SEEDS OF CHANGE

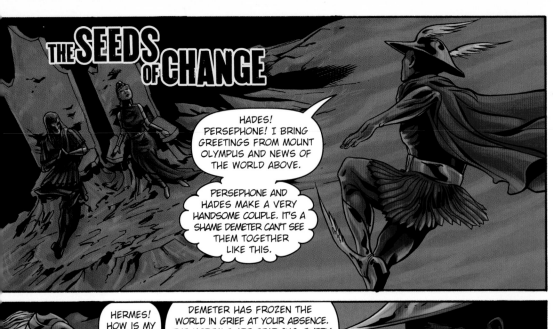

HADES! PERSEPHONE! I BRING GREETINGS FROM MOUNT OLYMPUS AND NEWS OF THE WORLD ABOVE.

PERSEPHONE AND HADES MAKE A VERY HANDSOME COUPLE. IT'S A SHAME DEMETER CAN'T SEE THEM TOGETHER LIKE THIS.

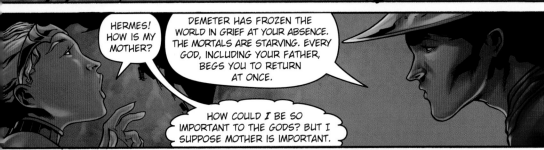

HERMES! HOW IS MY MOTHER?

DEMETER HAS FROZEN THE WORLD IN GRIEF AT YOUR ABSENCE. THE MORTALS ARE STARVING. EVERY GOD, INCLUDING YOUR FATHER, BEGS YOU TO RETURN AT ONCE.

HOW COULD *I* BE SO IMPORTANT TO THE GODS? BUT I SUPPOSE MOTHER IS IMPORTANT.

PERSEPHONE IS MY QUEEN! ZEUS *PROMISED* HER TO ME.

BUT HE DID NOT ASK DEMETER OR PERSEPHONE. SO THE MARRIAGE CANNOT BE.

I'D ALMOST FORGOTTEN HOW FRIGHTENING IT WAS TO BE GRABBED AGAINST MY WILL. HADES HAS BEEN SO KIND.

BUT I MUST GO BACK TO SEE MY MOTHER! WE CANNOT LET ALL THE MORTALS DIE FOR OUR LOVE.

PROMISE ME YOU WILL *RETURN!*

PLEASE.

IF I GO BACK, WILL MOTHER EVER LET ME RETURN? SHE CAN'T STOP ME! I'M A WOMAN NOW.

HERMES, WILL YOU GRANT US A FEW MOMENTS TO SAY GOODBYE?

OF COURSE.

WILL YOU WALK WITH ME IN THE ELYSIAN FIELDS, MY LOVE?

YES, MY KING.

I HOPE THIS WON'T BE FOR THE LAST TIME.

YOU KNOW HOW I FEEL ABOUT YOU, BUT IF YOU MUST GO, I WILL NOT TRY TO STOP YOU.

I MIGHT HAVE KNOWN HADES WOULD BE NOBLE. THAT MAKES IT EVEN HARDER FOR ME TO LEAVE.

SO, SHE DOES HAVE FEELINGS FOR ME!

I NEVER COULD HAVE IMAGINED YOUR WORLD HELD SUCH CHARMS. AND THAT YOU ...

BUT I MUST GO BACK TO MY MOTHER.

SURELY DEMETER CANNOT EXPECT YOU TO STAY A GIRL FOREVER. JUST AS WE ALL HUNGER FOR FOOD, WHEN WE MATURE, WE HUNGER FOR LOVE.

I DO LOVE HIM. BUT...

WON'T YOU SHARE THIS BEAUTIFUL FRUIT WITH ME?

I KNOW WHAT A POMEGRANATE MEANS— THE SYMBOL OF MARRIAGE AND FERTILITY. HE DOESN'T JUST ASK ME TO SHARE THE FRUIT; HADES ASKS FOR ME TO SHARE HIS LIFE.

SURELY YOU MUST BE HUNGRY AFTER ALL THIS TIME.

I DON'T KNOW WHICH TEMPTS ME MORE: THE LUSCIOUS FRUIT OR THE HANDSOME MAN!

THANK YOU, MY QUEEN! NOW WE SHALL BE TOGETHER FOREVER!

FOREVER! WHAT ABOUT MOTHER? SUNLIGHT? FLOWERS? CAN I ABANDON THE WHOLE WORLD ABOVE— EVEN FOR LOVE?

NO! I CAN'T! I'M SORRY, HADES. I CANNOT STAY HERE WITH YOU FOREVER.

I FEARED YOU WOULD REGRET SUCH A COMMITMENT. BUT I WILL MISS YOU!

I WILL MISS YOU, TOO, MY KING!

NO ONE MUST LEAVE!

THIS IS ZEUS'S COMMAND.

WHAT ABOUT MY FARE?

HE PAYS BY NOT DESTROYING YOU WITH HIS THUNDERBOLT.

IT'S NOT A COIN, BUT THAT WILL DO.

AT THE EDGE OF HADES' KINGDOM, PERSEPHONE SAW CHARON AGAIN.

THE FASTER YOU GO, THE SOONER WE SAVE ALL THE MORTALS FROM STARVING.

THAT WOULD MEAN A LOT OF COINS. BUT THERE'S NO RUSH. ALL WILL COME TO ME IN TIME.

GRRRRRR!

RRRRRRR!

GRRRROWL!

TAKE IT EASY, BOY! YOU REMEMBER PERSEPHONE, AND OF COURSE, YOU KNOW HERMES. LET THEM GO. EASY DOES IT!

DON'T FORGET ME, MY QUEEN!

SOON, PERSEPHONE WAS BACK IN THE SUNLIGHT ...

SO BRIGHT AND WARM! I'D ALMOST FORGOTTEN HOW WONDERFUL HELIOS IS.

BUT WHAT'S ALL THIS WHITE STUFF?

THIS IS WHAT HAPPENS WHEN THE WORLD FREEZES. WITHOUT YOUR MOTHER'S WARMTH, THE RAIN TURNED TO *SNOW*.

AND BACK IN HER MOTHER'S ARMS.

PERSEPHONE!

MOTHER!

ARE YOU ALL RIGHT? YOU LOOK THIN AND TIRED.

SO DO YOU!

YOU DIDN'T EAT ANYTHING, DID YOU? YOU KNOW THE RULES.

I HOPE SHE'LL UNDERSTAND.

I ATE A FEW POMEGRANATE SEEDS.

YOU WHAT?! YOU KNOW BETTER THAN THAT.

I KNOW, BUT ... I *LOVE* HIM.

THE POMEGRANATE PROBLEM

ZEUS SENT HIS MOTHER, *RHEA*, THE OLDEST OF THE GODS, TO TALK TO DEMETER.

SO, YOU SEE, IT SEEMS FAIR THAT PERSEPHONE SPEND A THIRD OF THE YEAR IN THE UNDERWORLD WITH HADES, AND THE REST OF THE YEAR HERE WITH YOU.

IF ONLY SHE HADN'T EATEN THOSE SEEDS!

PLEASE TELL ZEUS I PROMISE NOT TO FREEZE THE EARTH AGAIN, EXCEPT DURING THAT PART OF THE YEAR WHEN MY DAUGHTER WILL BE IN THE UNDERWORLD.

ONCE DEMETER KNEW HER DAUGHTER WAS NOT LOST TO HER FOREVER, SHE JOYOUSLY RESTORED THE FROZEN FIELDS TO THEIR FORMER GLORY.

IT'S LOVELY TO HAVE YOU BACK!

IT'S GOOD TO BE BACK.

AS IT WILL BE TO RETURN TO HADES—IN TIME.

THE UNDERWORLD ALSO CELEBRATED.

HOW'S THE BEST DOG IN THE UNDERWORLD? DID YOU MISS ME?

BOW WOW WOW!

WOOF WOOF WOOF!

ARF ARF ARF!

EVERYONE MISSED YOU, ESPECIALLY ME!

JUST BECAUSE I'M GLAD TO SEE HER DOESN'T MEAN THE QUEEN RIDES FREE.

-:SIGH:-
IT'S EVEN MORE BEAUTIFUL THAN I REMEMBERED.

SO ARE YOU!

42

SO EACH *WINTER*, PERSEPHONE RULED IN THE UNDERWORLD WITH HANDSOME HADES. AND EACH *SPRING*, WHEN THE SEEDS SPROUTED, THE EVER-YOUNG GODDESS RETURNED TO EARTH.

THE FIRST CROCUS!

PERSEPHONE IS BACK! OOH, I CAN'T WAIT FOR THE FESTIVAL.

THE GRATEFUL GREEKS CELEBRATED PERSEPHONE'S RETURN WITH ANOTHER FESTIVAL.

SOON THE FIELDS WILL BE FERTILE AGAIN!

THANKS TO DEMETER FOR THAT!

WE'LL BE UP TO OUR NECKS IN WORK, BUT AT LEAST WE'LL BE EATING.

I NEVER WANT TO GO THROUGH ANOTHER ENDLESS WINTER AGAIN.

FOUR MONTHS IS LONG ENOUGH, PRAISE THE GODDESS.

SO DEMETER REWARDED HUMANITY WITH THE KNOWLEDGE OF *AGRICULTURE*. DEMOPHOON, IN A CHARIOT PULLED BY SERPENTS, HELPED SPREAD THE KNOWLEDGE.

WINGED HORSES WOULD HAVE BEEN NICE, BUT THESE SERPENTS ARE FAST!

LIKE ALL WISE MOTHERS, THE GODDESS CAME TO ACCEPT SHARING HER DAUGHTER WITH A HUSBAND. AND THE GREEKS, LIKE ALL WISE PEOPLE, ACCEPTED THE BALANCE BETWEEN SPRING AND WINTER, LIFE AND DEATH.

SHE'LL ALWAYS BE MY LITTLE GIRL. BUT NOW PERSEPHONE IS ALSO A WIFE AND A QUEEN. NOT EVEN WE GODS CAN DEFY THE WAYS OF NATURE.

GLOSSARY

AMBROSIA: the food of the gods, made from divine substances. Humans sometimes made their own imitation ambrosia from honey, water, fruit, cheese, olive oil and barley (a grain).

APHRODITE: the Greek goddess of love

ARES: the Greek god of war

ATHENA: the Greek goddess of wisdom

CHARON: the boatman who guides souls across the River Styx into the underworld

DEMETER: the Greek goddess of the harvest and of agriculture

DEMOPHOON: the son of King Celeus and Queen Metaneira of Eleusis, taken care of as a child by Demeter

ELEUSIS: a city in Greece northwest of Athens, centre of the Eleusinian mysteries — sacred festivals dedicated to Demeter

ELYSIAN FIELDS: a beautiful part of the underworld where heroes and poets are sent after death

FURIES: the three female spirits, Tisiphone, Megara and Allecto, of justice and vengeance. Also known as the Erinyes, their job is to pursue wrongdoers.

HADES: the Greek god of the underworld

HERA: the Greek goddess of marriage and childbirth, married to Zeus

HERMES: the messenger of the gods on Mount Olympus

MOUNT OLYMPUS: the home of the Greek gods and goddesses

PERSEPHONE: Demeter's daughter, kidnapped by Hades

SHADES: the spirits of dead people who inhabit the underworld

STYX: the river that encircles the underworld. Once shades are ferried across the Styx by Charon, they cannot return to the world above.

UNDERWORLD: the kingdom of the dead, ruled by Hades

ZEUS: the main Greek god, the ruler of Mount Olympus

FURTHER READING AND WEBSITES

Blyton, Enid. *Tales of Ancient Greece* (Enid Blyton Myths and Legends) Element Books Ltd, 1998. All the famous stories are here, an inspirational collection of stories of love, treachery, foolishness, tragedy and humour.

Coats, Lucy and Anthony Lewis. *Atticus the Storyteller's 100 Great Myths* Orion Children's Books, 2003. A wonderful way to introduce children to the ancient world.

Deary, Terry. *Groovy Greeks* (Horrible Histories) Scholastic Hippo, 2007. This book adds a certain edge to the study of Ancient Greece by getting down to the nitty-gritty of Greek life and letting rip with the kind of nasty, revolting facts that any kids would kill to get their hands on.

Fanelli, Sara. *Mythological Monsters of Ancient Greece* Walker Books Ltd., 2002. Meet the living, fire-breathing mythical creatures of Greek legend.

MythWeb. http://www.mythweb.com/index.html. This site, with a searchable encyclopedia, provides students with information on gods, goddesses and places in Greek mythology.

Parker, Vic. *Ancient Greece* (Traditional Tales) Chrysalis Children's Books, 2004. Written with young readers in mind this title uses full-page colour illustrations to enhance tales of ancient times.

CREATING *DEMETER & PERSEPHONE*

In retelling this ancient story for modern readers, Justine and Ron Fontes drew upon classical and modern sources such as *Metamorphoses* by the Roman poet Ovid (43 BC–c AD 17), Edith Hamilton's *Mythology* and the *New Larousse Encyclopedia of Mythology*. Artist Steve Kurth used classical Greek art, such as painted vases and stone carvings, and anthropological sources to create the story's visual details. David Mulroy of the University of Wisconsin-Milwaukee ensured historical and visual accuracy.

original pencil sketch from page 30

INDEX

ABOUT THE AUTHORS AND THE ARTIST

JUSTINE AND RON FONTES met at a publishing house in New York City, USA, where Ron worked in the comic book department and Justine was an editorial assistant in children's books. Together they have written nearly 500 children's books, in every format from board books to historical novels. From their home in Maine, they also launched Sonic Comics with their first graphic novel *Tales of the Terminal Diner*. Other published projects include *The Trojan Horse: The Fall of Troy*, *Atalanta: The Race against Destiny* and *The Wooden Sword*. Lifelong library lovers, the Fonteses long to write 1,001 books before retiring to read.

STEVE KURTH was born and raised in west central Wisconsin, USA. He graduated with a BFA in illustration from the University of Wisconsin-Eau Claire. Steve's art has appeared in *Hercules: The Twelve Labours* and in numerous comic books, including *G.I. Joe*, *Micronauts*, *Ghostbusters*, *Dragonlance* and *Cracked* magazine.